First World War
and Army of Occupation
War Diary
France, Belgium and Germany

28 DIVISION
84 Infantry Brigade
Suffolk Regiment
1st Battalion
1 February 1915 - 20 October 1915

WO95/2277/3

The Naval & Military Press Ltd
www.nmarchive.com
Published in association with The National Archives

Published by

The Naval & Military Press Ltd

Unit 10 Ridgewood Industrial Park,

Uckfield, East Sussex,

TN22 5QE England

Tel: +44 (0) 1825 749494

www.naval-military-press.com

www.nmarchive.com

This diary has been reprinted in facsimile from the original. Any imperfections are inevitably reproduced and the quality may fall short of modern type and cartographic standards.

© Crown Copyright
Images reproduced by permission of The National Archives, London, England, 2015.

Contents

Document type	Place/Title	Date From	Date To
Heading	1st Battalion Welsh Regiment Jan 1915-October 1915		
Heading	28th Division 84th Infy Bde 1st Bn Welsh Regt Jan-Oct 1915		
Heading	28th Div. 84th Bde. War Diary. 1st Welsh Regt. January 1915.		
War Diary	West Downs School Winchester	16/07/1915	31/07/1915
Heading	28th Div. 84th Bde. Note. 84th Bde Came Under Order Of 5th Division. 22.2.15 War Diary 1st Welsh Regt. February. 1915		
War Diary		01/02/1915	07/03/1915
Heading	Maps.		
Miscellaneous	Tracing From Shewing Roughly Dispositions Of 1st Welch Regt In Left Sector Of Trenches At Zillebeke.		
Miscellaneous	Tracing From Map Shewing Roughly Trenches In Left Sector North Of Canal.		
Heading	5th Div. 84th Bde. War Diary 1st Welsh Regt. March 1915		
War Diary		27/02/1915	31/03/1915
Heading	28th Div. 84th Bde. Note. 84th Bde rejoined 28th Div from 5th Div. Apl 6/15 War Diary. 1st Welsh Regt. April 1915		
War Diary		01/04/1915	30/04/1915
Heading	28th Div. 84th Bde. War Diary 1st Welsh Regt. May. 1915		
War Diary		01/05/1915	31/05/1915
Heading	28th Div. 84th Bde. War Diary. 1st Welsh Regt. June 1915		
War Diary		01/06/1915	30/06/1915
Heading	28th Div. 84th Bde. War Diary. 1st Welsh Regt. July 1915		
War Diary		01/07/1915	31/07/1915
Heading	28th Div. 84th Bde. War Diary. 1st Welsh Regt. August 1915		
War Diary	In The Field.	01/08/1915	31/08/1915
Heading	84th Bde. 28th Div. 1st Welsh Regt. September 1915		
Heading	On His Majesty's Service.		
War Diary		01/09/1915	30/09/1915
Heading	84th Bde 28th Div. Embarked With Bde. for salonika 24.10.15 1st Welsh Regt. 1st to 20th October 1915		
Heading	On His Majesty's Service.		
War Diary		01/10/1915	01/10/1915
War Diary		01/10/1915	20/10/1915

1st BATTALION WELSH REGIMENT
JAN 1915 – OCTOBER 1915

28TH DIVISION
84TH INFY BDE

1ST BN WELSH REGT
JAN - OCT 1915

TO SALONIKA

28th Div.
84th Bde.

WAR DIARY.

1st WELCH REGT.

JANUARY.

1915.

Army Form C. 2118.

WAR DIARY
INTELLIGENCE SUMMARY
(Erase heading not required.)

Instructions regarding War Diaries and Intelligence Summaries are contained in F.S. Regs, Part II. and the Staff Manual respectively. Title pages will be prepared in manuscript.

Hour, Date, Place	Summary of Events and Information	Remarks and references to Appendices
8.50 a.m. 16th Jany/15. WEST DOWNS SCHOOL WINCHESTER.	Left Billets & proceeded by Rail to march to Southampton Docks arriving at 1:40 pm. Strength 26 Officers, 1 M.O. 49 of Sergts & Sergts 40 Corporals, 16 Drummers, 6 Buglers (of I.C.) 881 Ptes = total = 1019. (1 Officer & other ranks Billeting party, sent in advance, not included) Embarkation speedily carried out without hitch on R.M.S.S. "Cardiganshire". Only other troops on board were 60 men KING'S OWN (R. LANCASTER Regt) under Lieut Todd. At 6 pm moved out & anchored off NETLEY and remained there till 6 pm 17th January 1915.	
9.0 AM 18th Jany/15.	Arrived off Havre. Disembarked about 2 PM & formed up in large Cotton shed (No 6) QUAI de PONDICHERRY, where Battalion bivouacked for the night. 1 Skin Coat per man and 400 pints of Milk were issued to the troops. Weather fairly mild.	
8.15 AM 19th Jany/15 1.0 PM 20th Jany/15	Marched to Point No 3 & entrained. Train left at 1.0 PM. – Arrived at HAZEBROUCK & detrained & marched to billets at MERRIS – about 7 miles, arriving at 4.30 p.m. Rainy weather. Heavy roads.	1 man absent, 2 men sent to Hospital
26th Jany/15 28th Jany/15	Staff billets. Route marching. Daily route marches & instruction. Inspection by Field Marshal Sir John French, C-in-C	
20th Jany/15		Passed ... Lieut-Colonel M^c Wm Whitelock Comdg. 1/6 Mc Whitelock Reg^t

28th Div.
84th Bde.

Note:- 84th Bde came under
Order of 5th Division.
22.2.15.
....

WAR DIARY.

1st WELCH REGT.

FEBRUARY.

1 9 1 5.

Maps Attached:

Army Form C. 2118.

WAR DIARY
or
INTELLIGENCE SUMMARY
(Erase heading not required.)

Instructions regarding War Diaries and Intelligence Summaries are contained in F.S. Regs., Part II. and the Staff Manual respectively. Title pages will be prepared in manuscript.

Hour, Date, Place	Summary of Events and Information	Remarks and references to Appendices
1st February 1915.	Billets at MERRIS. Transport proceeded by road to VLAMERTINGE in the evening.	
2nd Feb. 1915.	Battalion (less transport) proceeded 1½ miles to STRAZEELE there taken on motor Buses to VLAMERTINGE. From there marched to YPRES. From YPRES Headquarters and right half Battalion marched to ZILLEBEKE (TUILERIES) and left half Battalion to BLAUWPOORT FARM in support of Northumberland Fusiliers and Cheshire Regiments respectively, the latter Battalion in first line trenches.	
3rd February 1915.	ZILLEBEKE & BLAUWPOORT FARM.	
4th February 1915.	In the evening Battalion took over 2nd line trenches from Northumberland Fusiliers.	
5th February 1915.	Battalion took over trenches North of YPRES – LILLE railway together with 1 Company Suffolk Regt who came under orders of Lieut Col Marden Commanding Left Section. Rough sketch of trenches attached. "A" "B" and "C" Grenadier Platoon had good trenches but portions of "B" were subject to enfilade and the finger held by the 2nd Grenadier Platoon was a dangerous one. They were never kept together by Lieut Evans-Jones whose gallant conduct in crawling outside his trenches and throwing hand grenades into the enemy's trenches	

WAR DIARY
or
INTELLIGENCE SUMMARY

(Erase heading not required.)

Army Form C. 2118.

Date, Place	Summary of Events and Information	Remarks and references to Appendices
	was brought to the notice of the G.O.C. 84th Brigade. "C" Coy had a very wet and disagreeable time of trenches, but suffered few casualties. Casualties :- "A" Killed or died of wounds. NIL Wounded 1 "B" NIL ---- 6 "C" 1 ---- 1 "D" NIL ---- 1	Lt. W.J.
6th February 1915	In trenches. - relieved during night 6/7 by Northumberland Fusiliers. Casualties - "A" Killed of died of wounds. NIL Wounded NIL "B" NIL ---- 1 "C" NIL ---- 1 "D" NIL ---- 1 Headquarters & A.B. returned to ZILLEBEKE and "C" and "D" Companies to YPRES.	W3
7th February 15.	A H.Ex explosive shell burst in the farm in which "B" Coy was located and set alight to a Barn in which there were some men. A good deal of Equipment burnt and 1 man killed and 7 wounded.	
8th February 15	In support. During night relieved the N. Fusiliers in trenches.	

Army Form C. 2118.

WAR DIARY
or
INTELLIGENCE SUMMARY
(Erase heading not required.)

Instructions regarding War Diaries and Intelligence Summaries are contained in F. S. Regs., Part II. and the Staff Manual respectively. Title pages will be prepared in manuscript.

Hour, Date, Place	Summary of Events and Information	Remarks and references to Appendices
9th February 15	In trenches. A portion of the trench had been given up by N. Fusiliers as untenable and trenches full. Casualties. [A: Killed or died of wounds 1. Wounded 5. / B: Nil — 4 / C: Nil — 2 / D: 1 — 3]	K 2. W 14
10th February 15	In trenches. During night relieved by North Fusiliers. Headquarters and Coys. companies to ZILLEBEKE and A and B Coys. to YPRES.	
11th February 15	In support till 6.30 p.m., when relieved by King's Own (Royal Lancaster) Regt. Marched to huts near MILLEKAPELLEN farm on VLAMERTINGHE – OUDERDOM road – about 7 miles to rest. Huts very bad, wet weather frost and very crowded. Total Casualties – 5th to 11th Feb. Officers – Nil Other ranks Killed 12 Wounded 34	
12.13th February 15	In huts at MILLEKAPELLEN.	

WAR DIARY
or
INTELLIGENCE SUMMARY

(Erase heading not required.)

Army Form C. 2118.

Hour, Date, Place	Summary of Events and Information	Remarks and references to Appendices
14th February 15	The Battalion was ordered at 1-30 p.m. in outpost of 85th Brigade and marched to YPRES. Orders received there that it was not required – Marched back arriving at 3.45 p.m. C.O. and 4 Company Commanders went to Cuy. Sgt. Major's mess to luncheon which Battalion was to occupy the near night. Cuy. Sgt. Major McCarthy dangerously wounded leaving Y trench and died later from wounds. Weather very wet and cold.	
15th February	The Battalion again marched out at 3-30 a.m. and marched through YPRES to the Chateau ROSENDAL about 1½ miles SOUTH of the town, marching out strength 24 officers 840 other ranks. Remained at the Chateau all day and at night relieved 3rd Royal Fusiliers in the left section of trenches North of the Canal. The track to the trenches was about 1½ miles and deep in holding mud. Y trench was on a sort of hillock and was capable of being made very strong, but there was a good deal of clear ground in front and a the N.q. it. It was regularly and accurately shelled though a day by the enemy. X trench was merely a series	See Sketch map.

WAR DIARY or INTELLIGENCE SUMMARY

Army Form C. 2118.

Hour, Date, Place	Summary of Events and Information	Remarks and references to Appendices
	of small dug-outs under a bank, these could be only 40 yards and could not be seen - it protected from small parties creeping in under cover of the Lisieux. Y Trench was merely a ditch with a very weak parapet and muddy close firs (40 yards) of the very strong German line. These were also times in advance of both flanks which gave trouble. The trench was traversed deep in water and crawling along the trench was not entering and leaving the trench. Y trench was not properly supported by fire from Z or T and was untenable. Z trench had been strong once, but was only partially held (see sketch). It was subject to enfilade fire from the village L. The parapets were not bullet proof and sand bags were shot down as soon as placed. "B" Company under Captain Montgomery and 2nd Generation Platoon were attached to the Right Sector S of the Canal. The enfilade fire in Z trench caused a portion of about 30 yards to be evacuated and a traverse built. The C.O. reported to Brigadier or Z and Y trench and proposed a retracted position.	
16" Feb. 15.		

WAR DIARY or INTELLIGENCE SUMMARY

Army Form C. 2118.

(Erase heading not required.)

Hour, Date, Place	Summary of Events and Information	Remarks and references to Appendices
17th Feb. 15.	Lieut Pope killed in Z trench, Lieut Lloyd in Y Trench, and Lieut Evan Jones in R Trench. Lieut Warner Davies wounded slightly whilst going into the trenches. Casualties: A. Killed or died of wounds 5, Wounded 10 B. — 1, — 1 C. NIL, — 1 D. — 1, — 3	K 3+7, W 1-15
18th Feb. 15.	Situation the same. Relieved during the night by 2nd Bn Cheshire Regt. Casualties: A. Killed or died from wds 4, Wounded 4, Missing 17 B. — 3, — 11 C. — 6, — 4 D. — 5, — 12 Battalion went to Chalôn Brendel. 136 men and Lieuts B.T. Phillips, Lomax & Brown sent to hospital with swollen feet — caused by wet trenches. During night 150 men used in digging a new line of trench — South of Canal and 150 in carrying rations to Cheshire Regt.	K 18- W 31, M 1 3:00
19th Feb. 15.	About 2 pm the G.O.C. 84th Bde instructed the C.O. to carry out his proposal for a retrenched line	

WAR DIARY or INTELLIGENCE SUMMARY

Army Form C. 2118.

Hour, Date, Place	Summary of Events and Information	Remarks and references to Appendices
20th Feb. 1915	North of the Canal. Work started at Dusk with 20 Grenadiers & 35 C. Company in New Trench B. 75 men had to be sent to Captain Montgomery which reduced the rifles in the left sector to 300 to hold a long designed and formerly manned by 400 rifles. Lieut Dundas sent out to reconnoitre a new line of trench S of the Canal was severely wounded and died later from his wounds. The Battalion relieving the 3rd Cheshire Regt in the trench. Capt L. Phillips wounded when entering trench. Lieut Douglas + 35 men C. Coy sent to Y Trench, as the new trench A could not be completed in time. Major A.G. Parteno left to assume Command of 2nd Battalion and Lieut Wells was transferred also. Good progress made with new trench B. till 9 a.m. when shelled by enemy. Men withdrawn to new trench A. K Coy scraped portion of Z trench – 35 men under Major Hogan. Report received from T trench at 11 am that 30 Germans had been seen running towards Y Trench	9/115

WAR DIARY or INTELLIGENCE SUMMARY

Army Form C. 2118.

(Erase heading not required.)

Hour, Date, Place	Summary of Events and Information	Remarks and references to Appendices
	and had been fired on. G. Sends were sent forward to see if Y trench was still held. A little later G. reports received from 2 trench that about 30 of the enemy had been seen in the avenues portion of 2 trench. Orders received by C.O. from G.O.C. 84th Inf. Brigade about 1 p.m. to turn enemy out with 1st Company of King's Own (Royal Lancaster) Regt. from 83rd Brigade and 1 Company 1st Numb. d Fusiliers also orders issued by Brigadier for attack to commence at 4.30 p.m. assisted by fire of Belgian artillery. The King's Own, supported on their right flank by 35 men of the Battalion under Major Loggan and fifteen Witherstone advanced in three lines with fixed bayonets. They ran up to within 30 yds of the trench ??? which was masked by tall broken stumps and tangled branches. The attack here held up by frontal and enfilade machine gun & by rifle fire. At 5.30 p.m. the G.O.C. 84" Infy Brigade arrives with 2 Northumberland Fusiliers and 2 Cheshire Regt and ascertained command. Report received in meantime that Y trench was not held by us.	4

WAR DIARY
or
INTELLIGENCE SUMMARY
(Erase heading not required.)

Army Form C. 2118.

Hour, Date, Place	Summary of Events and Information	Remarks and references to Appendices
	Casualties - Lieut Douglas and 34 men. C Company missing. Lieut Whitehorn wounded.	(= garrison of Y trench)
	A Coy. Killed or died of wounds. 5. Wounded 2. Missing NIL	K 15 W+37 M 1+37
	B Coy. " " 4 " 7 " NIL	
	C Coy. " " " " 15 " 37?	
	D Coy. " " " " 13. " NIL	
21st February 1915	Two attacks by 2nd N'umb Fusiliers at 12.30 am and 4.30 am failed. 3rd Cheshire found Y trench unoccupied by Germans and were ordered to hold new trench. A on whom in detail. Estimated casualties of K.own & 2nd N Fusiliers 150 each. Orders received for new trenches to be worked and connected with Z. Communication trench commences and after dark work carried on by 18th London Regiment. During night Battalion relieved by 1st Lincoln Regiment and marched to Infantry Barracks, YPRES. In the afternoon of this day Lieut Salmon dangerously wounded in the head.	Ypres

WAR DIARY
or
INTELLIGENCE SUMMARY

Army Form C. 2118.

(Erase heading not required.)

Instructions regarding War Diaries and Intelligence Summaries are contained in F. S. Regs., Part II. and the Staff Manual respectively. Title pages will be prepared in manuscript.

Hour, Date, Place	Summary of Events and Information	Remarks and references to Appendices
22nd February 15.	Total Casualties 16th to 22nd Feb. Killed or died of wounds 51. Wounded 86. Missing 41.	
23rd February 15.	In Infantry Barracks YPRES.	With Fifth Divn
	Battalion - 10 Officers 452 Other ranks marched to BAILLEUL 14 miles on transfer to 5th Division. [Commanded by Major General Morland C.B. D.S.O.] and went into billets in Rue de Cassel. Brigadier General Wilding CB admitted to hospital	
24th February 15.	Lieut Colonel (Temporary Brigadier General) L. J. Bols CB DSO assumed command of the 84th Infantry Brigade.	
25th-26th Feb 15	Battalion in Billets.	
27th Feb. 15.	Battalion 13 Officers 452 Other ranks marched out to East DRANOUTRE 4 miles to form reserve to Sector of trenches. Mostly C and D Coy in a farm on Mount Kemmel Road. A & B Companies in a farm on NEUVE EGLISE road.	

H. Morton
Lieut Colonel
Commanding 1st Batt. The Welch Regt.

WAR DIARY
or
INTELLIGENCE SUMMARY

(Erase heading not required.)

Army Form C. 2118.

Hour, Date, Place	Summary of Events and Information	Remarks and references to Appendices
27th February 1915	Battalion marched to DRANOUTRE at 2 p.m. – 3½ miles N.E. of BAILLEUL and went into billets in two farms as Reserve Battalion of the E Sector of defence DRANOUTRE Section	
28 Feb – 3 Mar 1915	At DRANOUTRE – Companies employed in making fascines and hurdles daily. Lieuts R. M. Earth and E. Newington and draft of 65 other ranks joined from Base ROUEN on 3 March. On night 3/4 March the Battn marched to the trenches – Head Quarters at Pond Farm. "A" & "C" Coys in trenches, "B" & "D" Coys in Support at COOKERS FARM.	
4 – 7 March 15	In trenches Companies relieved each other every 24 hours. Head Quarters changed to TEA FARM on 4 March. A very uneventful time.	

Casualties   Killed   Wounded   Missing

W.G.M.L.
"A" Coy   —   —   —
"B"   —   2   —
"C"   —   2   —
"D"   —   3   —
  —   2   1

M A P S.

Tracing from map shewing roughly
dispositions of 1st Welch Regt in Left Sector
of Trenches at ZILLEBEKE

FARM
Wald in Support

Hd Qrs. Supporting Battalion.

ILERIE

ZILLEBEKE

Brigade
HdQrs.

U Work

Second Line

D Support

Cavalry

C

B

A

Suffolk

1 Grenadiers

ZWARTELEEN

HILL 60

Scale 1/10,000

YDS 250 125 0 250 500 750 1000 YDS

Tracing from map showing roughly trenches in left sector NORTH of CANAL.

Fs Chapelle (Bn Hdqrs)

Dug outs Y&L Regt.
New Communication Trenches
Y&L Regt. 83° Bde.
NEW TRENCH B
NEW TRENCH A
TRAVERSE
M.G.S
LOCK
German trench
Abandoned portion of Z trench on which the attacks were made.
Canal flowing through cutting with wooded banks.
CANAL

Scale 1/10,000
YDS 250 125 0 250 500 750

5th Div.
84th Bde.

WAR DIARY.

1st WELCH REGT.

MARCH.

1915.

WAR DIARY
INTELLIGENCE SUMMARY
(Erase heading not required.)

Hour. Date. Place	Summary of Events and Information	Remarks and references to Appendices
27 February 1915	Battalion marched to DRANOUTRE at 2 p.m. — 3½ miles NE of BAILLEUL and went into billets in the farms at Reserve Battalion of the E sector of defend DRANOUTRE Section	
28 Feb – 3 Mar 1915	At DRANOUTRE — Companies employed in making fascines and hurdles, digging trenches. R.E. Smith and 8 Huntington and ? of 65 other ranks joined from 10th RWF on 3 March. On night 3/4 March the Bat'n marched to the trenches. Head Quarters at Pond Farm. A&C Coys in trenches. B&D Coys in support. Costers Farm in trenches. Companies relieved each other every 24 hours. Head Quarters charged to TEA FARM on 4 March A very uneventful time	Killed Wounded Missing A Coy 1 1 — B — 1 — C — — —

Army Form C. 2118.

WAR DIARY
or
INTELLIGENCE SUMMARY

(Erase heading not required.)

Instructions regarding War Diaries and Intelligence Summaries are contained in F. S. Regs., Part II. and the Staff Manual respectively. Title pages will be prepared in manuscript.

Hour, Date, Place	Summary of Events and Information	Remarks and references to Appendices
7th March 1915	Battalion relieved by E. Yorks Regt. and marched to former billets in BAILLEUL.	
8th–14th March 1915	In billets. 2/Lieut E.B. Llewellyn Jones and draft of 65 other ranks joined from Robin H’ds Capt F.E. Cooke and 9 other ranks joined on 13th March	2/Lieuts E.H.Lawley, E.Playfer, B.B Whitfield and H.A.C Yellen joined from ROUEN 12th March
14th March 1915	Marched at 10.30 a.m. to relieve 10th Infantry Brigade in PLOEGSTEERTE area. Billeted in two large farms at 6.0 p.m. ordered to stand by to march at short notice Northwards where heavy firing was heard - at 9'...	
15th March 1915	Remained in billets. In evening orders to relieve 10th Bde. in trenches given. Battalion all in firing line - some 1200 yds of front. Very good dry trenches [Lee Watts 'D' Coy wounded]	1.' 0.'
16–17th March 1915.	In trenches - One Casualty Relieved from 4 p.m. to 12 m.n. and ordered to march back to former billets at BAILLEUL - arrived 5am. 2/Lieut J.E. Coker and draft of 80 other ranks joined from ROUEN on 16th	
18–22nd March 1915.	In billets	
23rd March 1915.	Battalion marched to huts just S.o of LOCRE on road to DRANOUTRE.	

WAR DIARY
or
INTELLIGENCE SUMMARY

(Erase heading not required.)

Army Form C. 2118.

Hour, Date, Place	Summary of Events and Information	Remarks and references to Appendices

24th March 1915.	Relieved 2/5 Northumberland Fusiliers in E Sector Trenches DRANOUTRE area. Trench Strength 14 Officers 560 other ranks Head Quarters at LINDENHOEK Chalet. The Battalion was strengthened for trench duty by one Company 1st Monmouthshire Regt. Strength 4 Officers 176 other ranks.
	"C" Coy + 1 Platoon 1/Monmouth Regt in E trench
	"B" Coy + 2 Platoons 1/Monmouth Regt in 15 trench
	"A" Coy 1 Platoon in S.P.I
	2 Platoons 1/Monmouth Regt in POND FARM.
	"D" Coy less 1 Platoon in COOKER'S FARM
	"A" Coy less 2 Platoons in COOKER'S FARM.
	"A" Coy 1 Platoon } at Head Quarters
	"D" Coy 1 Platoon }
	Dressing Station POND FARM.
	
	Casualties Killed. Wounded 2. Missing.
	   "A" Coy. — 1 —
	   "B" Coy. — 1 —
	   "C" Coy. — 1 —
	   "D" Coy. — — —
	
	Very wet, ground very greasy.	

WAR DIARY or INTELLIGENCE SUMMARY

Army Form C. 2118.

(Erase heading not required.)

Instructions regarding War Diaries and Intelligence Summaries are contained in F. S. Regs., Part II. and the Staff Manual respectively. Title pages will be prepared in manuscript.

Hour, Date, Place	Summary of Events and Information	Remarks and references to Appendices
25th March 1915	In trenches. Began to freeze about midnight.	
26th March 1915	In trenches. Hard frost. Bomb exploded about midnight in E1 sight wounding 8 men including Coy. Sgt. Oates & broke telephone instrument. Casualties. Killed 3 Wounded 9 missing "A" Coy. — 1 — "B" Coy. — 5 — "C" Coy. 2 1 — "D" Coy. 1 3 — 2/Lieuts. J. Chamberlain, A.B. Covensmaker, C.E. Rumsey, Lt. Col. Herbert, and 13 other ranks joined from Rouen	
27th March 1915	In trenches. Frost continued. Head Quarters moved to PONDFARM. Dressing Station and 2 Reserve Platoons to PACK HORSE FARM. Casualties Killed 5 Wounded 12 missing "A" Coy. 1 4 — "B" Coy. 2 3 — "C" Coy. 2 3 — "D" Coy. — 2 —	

Army Form C. 2118.

WAR DIARY
or
INTELLIGENCE SUMMARY

(Erase heading not required.)

Instructions regarding War Diaries and Intelligence Summaries are contained in F.S. Regs., Part II. and the Staff Manual respectively. Title pages will be prepared in manuscript.

Hour, Date, Place	Summary of Events and Information	Remarks and references to Appendices
28th March 1915.	In trenches, frost continued. Relieved on night 28/29 March by 9th Northumberland Fusiliers and marched to huts at LOCRE. 2/Lieut J.E. Warren and draft of 60 other ranks arrived from ROUEN.	
29th March 1915.	In billets – still very cold – hard frost at night.	
30th March 1915	In billets. Battalion dug communication trench and dug-outs near FRENCHMAN'S FARM from 8.30 p.m. to 3 a.m. 31st.	
31st March 1915	In Billets	Cas. Month K & W 2 L, M 1

B. Marsden
Lieut – Colonel
Comdg 1st Bn The Welch Regt.

1247 W 3299 200,000 (E) 8/14 J.B.C. & A. Forms/C. 2118/11.

28th Div.

84th Bde.

Note:- 84th Bde rejoined 28th
Div from 5th Div. Apl 6/15.

;................

WAR   DIARY.

1st WELCH   REGT.

APRIL.

1 9 1 5.

WAR DIARY
INTELLIGENCE SUMMARY

(Erase heading not required.)

Army Form C. 2118.

Hour, Date, Place	Summary of Events and Information	Remarks and references to Appendices
1 April	Bn. relieves 2/N.Z. in trenches. Quiet night in E. sector- DRANOUTRE area. 1/ Manchester for tuft ran E.2, E.6, E.3. tE & trenches. Distribution - D. Coy E.1 + S.P, + 2 MGs B — 1S + MG C — 1S Support. Reserve at "E"D" Coy. Oosters Frm. A—Coy Paris Fm HQ Doulieu Fm. Crowthers.	
2 April	Weather - fine + frosty but dawned dull misty. Company in Reserve to lay at myft in ambush. B: relieved 83/BS trenches (D.A.S.) Coys repectively which were reserved by D+A. 2/3 rds Suffolk (as us) Crowthers	

WAR DIARY or INTELLIGENCE SUMMARY

Army Form C. 2118.

Hour, Date, Place	Summary of Events and Information	Remarks and references to Appendices
3 April	Saturday. "A" relieved "D" - "E", "8 Pl" & "B" relieved "C" in 1st Trench. BOC held Huts to Coy. [illegible]	No. & Names of Events in attached
4 April	Early D.B. - German showed white flag - several places but - enemies were just behind. With wire immed. sky. To our infantry. For relieved dawn. With 4/5 & 6 officers that all headed to safe. E & in which the Wing by 4° Brigstr [illegible] 5/1/ LOCKE. No casualties to state. Casualties	
5 - 13 April	In huts at LOCRE. On 2 April the B.C. was reviewed by Gen Sir H. Smith Dorrien GCSI Camg 2 Army. He addressed officers relative to Coy & Bn & Regiment, since amounts to flakes. Gen. had a Divisin. [illegible] Brigstr Gen [illegible] CO Lt Col [Challanger?] (? Gulley 4th) 2nd Bn PO [illegible]	

1247 W 3299 200,000 (E) 8/14 J.B.C. & A. Forms/C. 2118/11.

to face & have had no experience of trench warfare. They were so depleted as to have to be transferred to another Divn – the 3rd. Having now recruited they were to be retransferred to the 20th Divn. Since coming into the 5th Divn they had shown much energy & initiative & the GOC 5th Divn (Sir Charles Fergusson) had spoken in the highest terms of them & was sorry to lose them.

On 4 April the Bn was inspected by Sir Herbert Plumer Cmdg 5th Corps. He expressed himself very satisfied with the favourable reports received from the GOC II Corps, 5th Divn & 84 Bde as regards the Battalion & he confidently anticipated that in the fighting which would inevitably occur when the forward movement was made the Bn would maintain the reputation & high traditions which were associated with it.

A Draft of 50 Rk & Fl arrived this day at Vlamertinghe & awaited the arrival of the Bn.

WAR DIARY or INTELLIGENCE SUMMARY

Army Form C. 2118.

Hour, Date, Place	Summary of Events and Information	Remarks and references to Appendices
14 April	18n marches to Camp near Meteren	
15 —	In Camp - entertained 2 Canadians	
16 —	Nor up to hut. I rode W. of Ypres.	
17 "d"	Marched to Zunnebeke to relieve W.Y. = Feucher. Capt Polling (in command) Germans in Castle of ? been muse by the Nunenworks between trenches. Attaches with bombs & trumpet & drive them up & gave him back in turn to [word] Davis & [word] (words) 1st [word] Times. Ome sent up to help Any to the trenches if the tremens of trenches thepares) of what the news was like, to to the Efficiency of [word] Westgeenten kan used strings algorithm in attack Peckly the attack cars not take place till 2 a.m. After saved in which the Dam was lulled. 1st Herbert Cap? [word] (words) wounded. Alot, the sudden to attack with attillery support at 5 a.—

WAR DIARY or INTELLIGENCE SUMMARY

Army Form C. 2118.

Hour, Date, Place	Summary of Events and Information	Remarks and references to Appendices
18th	Owing to the Buffs lines having been charged a readjustment of the trench line + the attack and assault take till a dozen — when the guns open a rapid fire for 10 minutes after which the troops will both place along the trench in the trenches. The attack fails owing to this similar check the Germans has been aware of the attack — a small report afterwards shewn a wire entanglement — a trench has been constructed. The rest of the day passing quietly though it was thought it now cleared from our lines. The Buffs very tried with these circular trench which was dry from the night of the 18-19 + up on the the neighbour lines had attacked 7 Officers + 3 + OR Casualties. On McKenzie causing Casualties hand. On our German and Mauser fire	
19 – 20	Quiet	
21 –	At 5 p.m. the 16th ordered to make a front attack, retiring with some success.	We hold our own
22	After fight discovered that the Germans had evacuated the trench, and 7 Guns away opposite us found into a fire line at 7 Guns away.	

1247 W 3299 200,000 (E) 8/11 J.B.C. & A. Forms/C. 2118/11.

WAR DIARY
or
INTELLIGENCE SUMMARY
(Erase heading not required.)

Army Form C. 2118.

Hour, Date, Place	Summary of Events and Information	Remarks and references to Appendices
22	Indecisive bomb & rifle fire. At noon it was reported that the Germans were massing for an attack. Br. stood to. Our barrage rapidly suffocated came up as reinforcements. At 5 pm Germans fired before Stelling – another attempt. Heavy bombardment - no attack. Reinforcements returned 9 p.m. Syphus. At midnight shutter alarm - 2 x was given - 2 coys sent up - support which has happened. Casualties 17-22 with	
23-24	N.Y. relieves Br. in trenches.	
	At 4 pm. enemy at 3 am. 29. Stay fire keeps up for Alfranen (our ??? receives B 7 C to mench to Gipshoek) FREEZENBERG At 11 pm - extra marches at 12.15 am to more hols.	
25	Guns roar & went into dug outs. At 5 pm - Arts Gp sent to BOYNE ISEKE to support NZ B.	
26	Brunk heavy Shelles about to occur - Cyphu Menin ypres. Heavy fighting going on N of E of YPRES. B of A D.C. had fight with the rebels to NZ + ... Casualties -	

WAR DIARY
or
INTELLIGENCE SUMMARY

(Erase heading not required.)

Army Form C. 2118.

Hour, Date, Place	Summary of Events and Information	Remarks and references to Appendices
27.	Reports hand Stellos - Casualties	No dropouts made of night
28.	Hear Stella again. 2/Lt Breth wounded. German aeroplane brought down over now.	
	A/c returns to Dropouts from N.D.	
29.	A quiet day	
30.	Stellos again - Ayshelehr message to droops "B dt" from Lut J Aird received.	

28th Div
84th Bde.

WAR DIARY.

1st WELCH REGT.

MAY.
1915.

WAR DIARY
or
INTELLIGENCE SUMMARY.
(Erase heading not required.)

Army Form C. 2118.

Place	Date	Hour	Summary of Events and Information	Remarks and references to Appendices
	Nov		Shells again - heavy but be counted	
	1		8" rounds to hear line of trenches very if apart	
	2		Counter-attacks	
			& eighth heavy howitzers which were not - shells fuel heavy	
	3		10' tel 18' in fact trenches untaken - 16: eight howitzers	
	4		all night - pour transfer & a great scarcity of cartridges	
			our SOS rockets on left of tel 2 a.m that half line has gone	
			Ammn to Leas pumps - fact General orders to keep	
	#		On same the targets. Her SOS usfortackle & Kellas counterattack	
			fearful - Cannulles -	

WAR DIARY or INTELLIGENCE SUMMARY

Army Form C. 2118.

Hour, Date, Place	Summary of Events and Information	Remarks and references to Appendices
5—	Very heavy shelling to peal of "A" Coy trench Casualties—	
6—	Much quieter — relatively M.D. arrived G.O.R. we to suffer + a.a. stores &	
7—	from as Lam fire ceased. Replies extremely ill D? At 7.15p — A Coy sent up to D5 + hits back or left of D7? Shys C.O. attack on our trenches. left flank of treats of 83 Rifle Broken by concentrated shell fire, being right	
8.	of 15 S.R. exposed. Enemy press'd on to position. Infantry. + 64-95 th Confederacy units Coy hur. Reinforced on Checking up 84-95 th. occupies G.O.R. line. Cut per fire fire. On occupies 3 - 5 p —	
9—	G.O.R. line. Very heavy shelling. Casualties. trenches with R. Warwicks who occupies G.O.R.	
10.	Exchange w. Divine, here, remainder to reserve. Smith 2i Coy in Dis. line. Relieved at 11 p-m by 83 Bde. Marchd back to huts	

WAR DIARY
or
INTELLIGENCE SUMMARY
(Erase heading not required.)

Army Form C. 2118.

Hour, Date, Place	Summary of Events and Information	Remarks and references to Appendices
11th	Neuter Left 5pm for huts 16 farms west just E	just E of Ypres
12th	Ypres. Marched at 5pm to farms 2 miles SW of Ypres	
13th	At rest in farms.	
14th	Composite Brigade formed as follows. 1 Bn 4/ Cheshire Regt. 1 Hoses 3/ Mon. Headquarters Staff in, 1/ Cheshire Regt 2/ Buffs, 1 York & Lancaster Regt — Moved back to billets nr Vlamertinghe Lt Col Maxwell CMG as temporary Commander of Brigade Major Stoke assumed Command of Battalion	
15th	Moved to fresh billets in farm near Poperinghe Depot 3 officers and 215 other ranks joined the Battn. Principally from 5/SWB — Discipline & Disipline of Depot Bad — Marching bad — in billets.	
16		
17 – 18	Battalion marched to Herzeele. Billeted in farms	
19	at Herzeele	
20 – 21st	Battalion marched back to Vlamertinghe.	
22nd	Took our turn in the firing line country near Hooge. Marching of the new draft very bad.	

WAR DIARY or INTELLIGENCE SUMMARY

Army Form C. 2118.

Hour, Date, Place	Summary of Events and Information	Remarks and references to Appendices
23rd	In Trenches Dept? So N.O.T. Men arrived.	
24th	Battalion relieved by 11th Hussars - Marched back to Baizan. Were carried H.A.on - Ordered out again at 11.30 as Cavalry had lost ground owing to being gassed. Rested near Ypres till Noon. Orders to advance about 12.30. Heavily shelled. Crossing Canal (Square H.13.A.8) 6 officers + about 30 men transport. Advanced along Zone Railway to Square I 16.A. Heavily shelled. Lt. Col. Marden however kept Batt. together. Command = 8th Brigade ordered to attack enemy holding Trenches near BELLEWARDE FARM (I.2.A.A.). Advanced about 3 Coys towards heavy stream firm, in the line. Advanced keep towards MENIN Road - Heavy rifle fire - numerous casualties. Reached a point in Square I 17.A.8. finding remainder of Brigade had not come up. Remained there intended at edge of wood in I.18.B. The Regt heavy. Captain L. Phillips killed here. Made a second advance about 8.15 but could not very well further. At 12.30. 0m. The Brigade was ordered to reform on the No 12 point of MENIN Road near WITTE POORT FARM, and attack. Take the hut to the BELLEWARDE position. Coys tried to go on & Brigade on the right. Other Stations Soon after I, but the assault was given away, & by our own Kraft in the trenches on the railway Who had been evidently told to co-operate by fire. A Rifle fire has pinned by Germans with Rifle asst from numerous concealed machine guns. Major Toke, Captains Arthur Westly, 2/Lieuts Bryan & Ramsey	

WAR DIARY or INTELLIGENCE SUMMARY

Army Form C. 2118.

Hour, Date, Place	Summary of Events and Information	Remarks and references to Appendices
25th	Advanced through Railway line from Spanr. 1.K.R. - Quite a tough job to top of the hill. Has Charged at the point of the bayonet and the Germans driven out of a trench at the top. Captain Westby was killed and 2/Lieut. Ramsey wounded here. 2/Lieut. Poulton has been wounded down. Under a very heavy fire. the Casualties being numerous. Been our own artillery opened fire on the hill. Everything our men & some ? the Cheshire Regt. Shropshire & Somersets got out about 50 to evacuate the hill. The remainder of the Battalion together with the Shropshires - Northumberland Fusiliers Attached to Battalion from the East of the road in front of WATTREPORT FARM but to fire from the German machine guns was so Terrific, and little - no support was given by the 8th Brigade on the right, that they were forced to fall back. The losses in the Regt. were heavy - Between officers 3 killed, 11 wounded. 1 missing. Other ranks 11 killed 141 wounded 266 missing. The missing are in all probability are killed as no prisoners have been taken as far as is known. Officers killed. Captain & Adjutant E M Westby L. Phillips Topham Duke of Cornwall	

WAR DIARY
or
INTELLIGENCE SUMMARY

(Erase heading not required.)

Army Form C. 2118.

Instructions regarding War Diaries and Intelligence Summaries are contained in F. S. Regs., Part II. and the Staff Manual respectively. Title pages will be prepared in manuscript.

Hour, Date, Place	Summary of Events and Information	Remarks and references to Appendices
25th	Officers missing Captain C.C. Tortington Officers Wounded Lieut. Col. T.O. Marden Captain Montgomery " Yeats Rumsey (missing) Munro, Daring, Clayton " Baggally, Lunn, Dart, Jones, Carter. Returned by Royal Scots and Marines back to bivouac in Bazaoun Road.	
26 - 27	In Balloon Ravine	
28th	Brigade marched to HERZEEH	
29th	Inspection by General Allenby. — Great Parade given to the magnificent work done by 88th Brigade. Draft of 99 men arrived, = Lieut. bradley attached to 5th Plant Shelters in deception.	R.T. 10th Bryn Came as 1/5th. 2/6 Essex Regiment.
30th - 31st	N. Alect to HERZEET.	

1247 W 3299 200,000 (E) 8/14 J.B.C.& A.   Forms/C. 2118/11.

28th Div.
84th Bde.

54

WAR DIARY.

1st WELCH REGT.

JUNE

1915.

Army Form C. 2118.

WAR DIARY
or
INTELLIGENCE SUMMARY
(Erase heading not required.)

Instructions regarding War Diaries and Intelligence Summaries are contained in F.S. Regs., Part II. and the Staff Manual respectively. Title pages will be prepared in manuscript.

Hour, Date, Place	Summary of Events and Information	Remarks and references to Appendices
1-2ⁿᵈ Jan	Billet at HERZEEL	
3ʳᵈ	Brigade Paraded on King's birthday	
4ᵗʰ	Draft of 90 men arrived	
6ᵗʰ	2/Lieut HARRISON, RAWLINS, HORE & WARREN & DAWE. 2/Lieut LEFF & BATTEN joined the Battⁿ	
7ᵗʰ. 9ᵗʰ	In billets at HERZEEL	
10ᵗʰ	Brigade route march	
11ᵗʰ	Left HERZEEL & marched to RHENINGFELS. In huts for the night.	
12ᵗʰ	Left for DICKEBUSH - Batt. bivouac in East. Front about 1½ miles East. 2/Lt Daws Hospital accidentally wounded	
13ᵗʰ. 17ᵗʰ	In Battn. Brigade reserve in RIDGE WOOD. Battalion employed in digging every night. Majr MORGAN joined on 14ᵗʰ	
18ᵗʰ	Relieved from front Regiment in trenches. Trenches kept breastworks. Required in trenches. More than any. & bullet proof	
19ᵗʰ. 20ᵗʰ	In trenches - no casualties - 2/Lieut WEBER joined on the 20ᵗʰ	
21ˢᵗ	In trenches. 1 man wounded on 20ᵗʰ	

WAR DIARY
or
INTELLIGENCE SUMMARY
(Erase heading not required.)

Army Form C. 2118.

Hour, Date, Place	Summary of Events and Information	Remarks and references to Appendices
22nd June	Lieut. Col. Rev. Nixon killed firing over parapet - Bureia outside RIDGE WOOD. near GORDON FARM. 2/Lieut BEWICK LORD joined Battalion.	Map. VOORMEZEELE 1/10,000
23rd "	Head Quarters moved from GORDON FARM to Dug-out near BRASSERIE.	
24th "	Heavy Shower during day, 2 men wounded.	
25th "	Thunderstorm with heavy rain. Communication trenches knee deep in water.	
26th "	Enemy Shelter trenches with "Whiz-bang" Shells, A. Cy. relieved by Monmouth Regt.	
27th "	Remainder of Battn. relieved by 4/Suffolk Regt. Battn. bivouacked in RIDGE WOOD -	
28th "	Battalion in RIDGE WOOD. 300 men employed in digging in vicinity of Tunnelers Officers reconnoitred Reserve trenches -	
29th "	Battalion in RIDGE WOOD. 300 men employed digging with Main Entrance reconnaissance - Man killed, 1 man wounded the BOIS CARRÉ.	
30th "	Do. Do. Do. 2 men wounded -	

Do A R Hoggan Major
Commanding 1 S.Wales Borderer Regiment

28th Div.
84th Bde.

WAR DIARY.

1st WELCH REGT.

JULY.

1 9 1 5.

WAR DIARY or INTELLIGENCE SUMMARY

Army Form C. 2118.

Hour, Date, Place	Summary of Events and Information	Remarks and references to Appendices

15th July, 1915

3°° — Batt. in RIDGE WOOD. Two men employed in digging. Officer continued digging reinforcing Reserve line. Two men were still digging 2½.

4th, 5th, 6th, 7th, 8th, 9th — 2/Lieut. Bradbury & Davies came as draft of 120 O.R. Joining the Battalion.
Sergt Hickock hit a very light off into his face — Is afraid lost both eyes.
In Trenches VOORMEZEELE VIERSTRAAT. A Quiet tour of duty. Casualties 18 wounded — one rifle grenade killed two men, wounded six on the 9th.

10th — Left the Trenches and moved to Canada Huts near DICKEBUSH.

11th — Day of rest. Played the 6th Welch at Rugby football. 1 Welch/42 that 6th Welch, goal try.

13th — Again moved to huts NW of LA CLYTE called ROSEN HILL BECK. Lt Moir appointed Machine Gun officer

14th — Day of rest. WEST OUTRE — Lt J. Pullen went to Hospital.

15th — Marched to Trenches near KEMMEL near LINDENHOEK Cross Road.

16th — Quiet day but one man killed & one mortally wounded. Shooting over parapet. Major Toke went to Hospital. During this tour 2 men were killed, 10 wounded.

17, 18, 19 — Left Trenches and went into huts at LOCRE. This was a very restful place. The Officers had a good rest — men smartened up — Had a Battalion Parade on the 23rd.

20, 21, 22 —

23, 24, 25, 26, 27 — In Trenches KEMMEL near LINDENHOEK Cross Road again on 23rd. 2/Lt Captain Hobbs & Lt Hooper joined the Battalion. Quiet tour of duty — Nothing noteworthy to report. The following Casualties occurred. 23 — One one four wounded. 26 — 1 killed 1 wounded.

WAR DIARY
or
INTELLIGENCE SUMMARY
(Erase heading not required.)

Army Form C. 2118.

Hour, Date, Place	Summary of Events and Information	Remarks and references to Appendices
July 28th 29.30.31	No Casualties. Left for rest at Loos. Quiet. Morning of 30th Alarm Stand to at 3.30am owing to lively fire attack at 200yds — Dismissed 4.30 — Quiet time at LOCRE — We had sports and several games of Rugby, a good game with the 6th Welch which ended in a draw. O.F. Hoggan Major Comdg 1 The Welch Reg 31/8/16	

28th Div.
84th Bde.

WAR DIARY.

1st WELCH REGT.

AUGUST

1 9 1 5.

WAR DIARY or INTELLIGENCE SUMMARY

Army Form C. 2118.

(Erase heading not required.)

Instructions regarding War Diaries and Intelligence Summaries are contained in F. S. Regs., Part II. and the Staff Manual respectively. Title pages will be prepared in manuscript.

August

Hour, Date, Place	Summary of Events and Information	Remarks and references to Appendices
August In the Field. 1st 2nd 3rd	August 1st Church Service at 10am. 1st The Welch; 6th Welch; 1st Suffolks On the 2nd left for Trenches near KEMMEL G1; G2; G3; G4; H1 Head Quarters Doctors House - KEMMEL The 3rd was uneventful.	
4th	On the evening of the 4th about 8.45pm the enemy exploded a mine in G1. Three Trenches were destroyed burying 17 men. Captain Egerton, Lt Weber organised a rescue party. This party behaved with great coolness and gallantry and dug out under fire 16 men alive — one dead — one man was received 16 hours afterwards alive — The remainder could not be found. The braves and devotion to duty are especially words of Captains Egerton, Lt Weber, Sgt Reynolds Regt Prev. also Frank Bonsy's & pt Shelton Black J. Hopkins; Thomas, Truly - L/C Cpl Shelton Lance Corporal Bancroft, who was stunned, assisted the head was uncovered, began crying encouraging the party men. During this time it took to dig him out. The attack was attended with vigour.	

WAR DIARY
or
INTELLIGENCE SUMMARY

Army Form C. 2118.

Hour, Date, Place	Summary of Events and Information	Remarks and references to Appendices
August 5th	Quiet day. In the evening enemy Sheaved Chewing Sergt Sheeg captured the men but lost over the parapet, butchering himself two shot through the head - killed two of the Sergeants who came from India with us	
August 6	Sixth Seventh were quiet on the night of the 8th there was a heavy artillery fire from our guns to drive fire away from Hooge which was being attacked by us. The Hooge attack was very successful so reply from artillery fire but trenches were shelled in the afternoon of the 8th. Casualties 2 killed 9 wounded	
9th	Came out of Trenches and went for rest to Kimmel LOCRE Bady or huts.	
10, 11, 12, 13	Restful days then cleaned up for battle and killed together with Corporals and dined to several Games of Bridge &c. Well played — We defeated the 1st Welsh	
14 15 16 17	Left Locre for Kemmel Shelters remained here for two days and then returned to Trenches at KEMMEL on the 17th	
18	One man killed, put his head over the parapet too much. Shot	
19 20	On the 19th The Corps Commander visited the Trenches some Casualties one killed four wounded	

Army Form C. 2118.

WAR DIARY
or
INTELLIGENCE SUMMARY
(Erase heading not required.)

AUGUST

Hour, Date, Place	Summary of Events and Information	Remarks and references to Appendices
1 to 24th August	Some special reports were made during this period in G.1 & G.3 Trenches. These were made in conjunction with Curtain Holts. Along with Lieut Pewringford 2 Dorsey, 2t Pullen, 2t Bradbury, 2t McDougal. On the 16th & 5th & 7th summer were gallery blown up. There was shelled — Trench Overshaked with "Jomis 22 & 23. Enemy saptence were very near Guys & but over own portion. On 24th at 2 am enemy shelled trenches for over G1 & G2 which we hold the parts in G1 to 10 pm. There was shell & rifle fire so violent for quite a long time On effort Lieut Pullen and 50 other Rank volunteered to repair the damage done. Sorry to say the officer and only 2 hours sent on the 24th was, brought the officers having only 2 hours sent on the 24th Lieut Bradbury with stretcher parties especially well. Lt Bradbury was refusing from a hotly pressed pit when his pass got flung pitfall when one of the trenches had to refuses to go sick to was wounded some work of the to come out of the trenches.	There were some 30 casualties on the company during the tour
25.9	6.00 to Baileys hut LOCRE	Mess: Yate, Uniacke & Kerr Lt Col Boynoulins Lut Cupp: Jeffs & Uniacke, 2 in command

Army Form C. 2118.

WAR DIARY
or
INTELLIGENCE SUMMARY

(Erase heading not required.)

AUGUST

Hour, Date, Place AUGUST	Summary of Events and Information	Remarks and references to Appendices
26th - 28th	General clean up & baths for the men. Defects in month Reg'l also game of rugby	
29th - 30th - 31st	Moved to KEMMEL SHELTERS. Men employed digging at night on Suidon's line of defence. One man wounded. Visible digging	Lt. Kerr R.A.M.C. left us & Lt. Brockes relieved him.
	Casualties August	
	10 men killed + 40 wounded.	

A.H.H.H. Dryer
Commanding 1/Hert Reg.

84th Bde.
28th Div.

1st WELCH REGT.

SEPTEMBER

1 9 1 5

On His Majesty's Service.

1st Bn Wiltshire Regiment SEPT 1st - OCT 20th

Army Form C. 2118.

WAR DIARY
or
INTELLIGENCE SUMMARY
(Erase heading not required.)

Instructions regarding War Diaries and Intelligence Summaries are contained in F. S. Regs., Part II. and the Staff Manual respectively. Title pages will be prepared in manuscript.

Hour, Date, Place	Summary of Events and Information	Remarks and references to Appendices
SEPTEMBER		
September 1	At Trenches near KEMMEL. Run up to B2 trenches. Defensive fire - no damage. Shells - no damage.	Captain A. H. Watts promoted to Major.
2, 3, 4	Quiet in Trenches - another hung flare up in B2 - no casualties. Yes, we expected the dust from the passing Trench fire settled down. Mons 2 platoon head settled down.	Lieutenant Penruck wounded in the head (slight) 3rd Sept.
5	Returned to KEMMEL Shelters.	
6	MOAT LOCRE	
7	Usual ideas as Run and for NCOs & men.	
	3rd an French Con = 2 - firing inspired the Regt down by the Major	
	an first place with an inspection	
	Ser to KEMMEL SHELTERS stopt the Bn was digging at night	
	1 man killed & 1 wounded.	
	R.E.	
	... support in completing C.12.5 Trenches SP y 16	
	12 Shelters on mile from hill 2 wounded.	

Army Form C. 2118.

WAR DIARY
or
INTELLIGENCE SUMMARY
(Erase heading not required.)

Instructions regarding War Diaries and Intelligence Summaries are contained in F.S. Regs., Part II. and the Staff Manual respectively. Title pages will be prepared in manuscript.

Hour, Date, Place	Summary of Events and Information	Remarks and references to Appendices
SEPTEMBER		
13th	Situation normal. Lt. Col. Morgan went on a few days leave to England. Major Moffitt took over command.	? wounded
14th	Situation the same except for some slight shelling. 2nd Lieut. Jolles returned from sick leave.	4 wounded
15th	Slight shelling again. Three officers from Army reported for trench instruction for 24 hrs.	? wounded
16th	Nothing out of the ordinary took place during the 24 hrs	
17	2nd Lieut. Attlay (M.E. + Phungnel) shelled BLACK REDOUBT for about 1 hour, the enemy replied with 8" into our "F" trenches which were held by "C" Company, some 40 rounds were fired, but no casualties. Came out of trenches and marched to KEMMEL SHELTERS. Lt. Col. Morgan returned from leave. 2nd Canadian Div: withdrawing from front line.	
18th	Moved to LOCRE. 3rd Canadian Bde on way through to relieve our Bde	
19th	Remained at LOCRE	
20th	Route march. Relief of Bdes effected.	
21st	Bde marched to PRADELLES, where we were billeted in farms. Bn. marched some 10½ miles + a hot day. 16 men fell out.	

Army Form C. 2118.

WAR DIARY
or
INTELLIGENCE SUMMARY

(Erase heading not required.)

Instructions regarding War Diaries and Intelligence Summaries are contained in F. S. Regs, Part II. and the Staff Manual respectively. Title pages will be prepared in manuscript.

Hour, Date, Place	Summary of Events and Information	Remarks and references to Appendices
SEPTEMBER		
22nd	General clean up.	
23rd	Route march etc.	
24th	Pradelles	
25th	Pradelles	
26th	Marched at 8 a.m. Through Merville to PARADIS & billeted there for the night.	
27th	Battalion bivouaced to BETHUNE at 9.30 a.m. & then marched to MAZELLES & bivouacked.	
28th	Moved to SAILLY & bivouacked.	
29th	Battalion went into support at VERMELLES.	
30th	Battalion went into support of 21st Brigade behind HULLOCH. Relieved at 4 p.m. & returned to LANCASTER TRENCH at VERMELLES.	

84th Bde
28th Div.

Embarked with Bde. for Salonika 24.10.15.

1st WELCH REGT.

1st to 20th OCTOBER

1 9 1 5

On His Majesty's Service.

Army Form C. 2118.

WAR DIARY
or
INTELLIGENCE SUMMARY.
(Erase heading not required.)

Instructions regarding War Diaries and Intelligence Summaries are contained in F. S. Regs., Part II. and the Staff Manual respectively. Title pages will be prepared in manuscript.

Place	Date	Hour	Summary of Events and Information	Remarks and references to Appendices
	OCTOBER 1st		At 3 p.m. the Battalion would proceed to attack LITTLE WILLIE. The attack took place at 5 p.m. The following is an account written by Major Hoggan. On the 1st October the _ of the hotel Regiment were ordered to take a trench called LITTLE WILLIE at the point of the bayonet regardless of all costs.	

1247 W 3299 200,000 (E) 8/14 J.R.C. & A. Forms/C. 2118/11.

WAR DIARY or INTELLIGENCE SUMMARY

Army Form C. 2118.

Hour, Date, Place	Summary of Events and Information	Remarks and references to Appendices
1st October 1915 (Cont'd)	LITTLE WILLIE is a Trench in continuation of HOHENZOLLERN REDOUBT to the North. The 6th Welch Regiment, commanded by Lt Colonel Lord Ninian Crichton Stuart, occupied the trench called "THE OLD BRITISH LINE", obtained in part of "LITTLE WILLIE" and 300 yards distant from it, at 7pm. The WELCH REGT. were in position in this trench. Yesterday were a ridge from which we had been unable to see, and to now up again in the absence of Lt P Hogan who had been in command since 18th June. The O.C. Lieut Colonel L.P. Hogan who had been in command since 18th June — Col. Marden C.M.G. having been wounded in May — assembled the Officers, explained the situation — everyone watched very carefully and orders were given. — "Leaving at 8 P.M. Climb over the parapet" (Buda who had been assumed) "have formed in perfect silence, move in quick time, keep time" — The thing was perfectly perfect, at 8pm the 1st WELCH crept over the parapet the one man by piece in line into no man's. The second in command, Major HOBBS, and O.C. WELCH in the centre of the line. So silently was the advance carried out, that the Regiment was within 100 yards of the enemy before they discovered. Then from both flanks machine guns opened fire + the whole length of the Officers trench opened rapid fire. The Commander, Officers were sang out "Forward 41st - Let at em Welch"! In 20 sec. there were 250 men + a proportion of Officers on the floor! The remainder were in the Trench bayonetting those in the Trench and firing at the retreating Prussian Guards. It was a fallen Little affair, but also, Two serious mishaps then occurred. (a) The attack did not prolonged for enough to the left, leaving six bays of Trench (about 50 Germans) on the left flank, still in possession of the Germans (b) The Coy. on the right had lost touch and upon of 40 yards occurred. This gap gave the Trench in front them, but left 40 to 50 Germans in occupation between them and the right of the WELCH line. In occupying the Trench men at once went to consolidate the position against Counter attacks. The Germans on both flanks started bombing. —	

Forms/C. 2118/11.

WAR DIARY
or
INTELLIGENCE SUMMARY

(Erase heading not required.)

Army Form C. 2118.

Hour, Date, Place	Summary of Events and Information	Remarks and references to Appendices
14th October 1915 (cont)	The supply of bombs was very limited, about 600 — the attack not having been prolonged far enough to the left arrived. The Regiment of the communication trench laden to the supports — thus they were cut off from supplies too & water — & worst of all bombs. Volunteers were called for to go back & bring bombs, two more bombs were secured. Written messages were sent back to the supports — carried by a reliable officer so that there would be no miscarriage (Capt Gerster carried the message). (1.) Supports were asked for on the right of the position to connect up with the company on the right — only 50 men arrived with one officer — they came into the trench without fighting leaving the right still isolated. (2nd) Supports were sorely for the left of the position to push the enemy out — the bayonet from his position in the trench — two men not complied with, an officer was sent to Brigade Headquarters to explain situation. A communication trench was in course of construction towards the middle of the trench — the 8th Welch worked hard all night at the trench superintended by Lord Ninian — The /Welch digging hard given them —ible to meet these diggers. The trench was not completed by 2.30 p.m. A messenger was to have aeros the 20 yards yet to be dug was shot. Hit three in two shots showing the enemy was	

WAR DIARY or INTELLIGENCE SUMMARY

Army Form C. 2118.

(Erase heading not required.)

Hour, Date, Place	Summary of Events and Information	Remarks and references to Appendices
2nd October 1915	We aware of the situation. The stold right & morning were spent in bombing battles on each flank. He held the best of these battles, wounding or taking prisoners. — By 10 A.M. the bombs were exhausted — the enemy's supply were unlimited. The situation was now serious. Having now no bombs to reply the enemy moved up gradually from both flanks. There were now about 40 wounded all lying about in the trench. The enemy opened with minenwerfer shells — Two to that soldiers call "Sausage up". He still having reached the distance it is regulated for drop perpendicularly down & can be seen all the way & can be dodged. — The men were now so congested it was hopeless to get out if the way. — Major HOBBS, second in command, was magnificent, cool & collected, he held the men together & kept their spirits up in a wonderful manner. At 2-30 p.m. a third German bombing party attacked in the centre, coming down a communication trench from their main position. The Officers commanding & Major Hobbs, collected some men together, leading them with rifle & fixed bayonets, charged	

WAR DIARY
or
INTELLIGENCE SUMMARY

(Erase heading not required.)

Army Form C. 2118.

Instructions regarding War Diaries and Intelligence Summaries are contained in F. S. Regs., Part II. and the Staff Manual respectively. Title pages will be prepared in manuscript.

Hour, Date, Place	Summary of Events and Information	Remarks and references to Appendices
2nd October 1915 (Cont'd)	changed. This Bombing party, a party of bombs destroyed & a scattered the men following. Both flanks were being pushed into the centre. The word was given to move one man at a time to the rear Communication trench. Machine guns opened fire upon the men. The Bombers retired up. The 6th Welch then made preparation to stop this rush of bombers by opening rifle & machine gun across traverse after traverse. Enemy shewed very strong resistance and that dead while throwing and directing fire from ? his machine guns. The 1st Welch again occupied the old British front lines (the 6th Welch holding the new trench) and remained in occupation for 24 hours. These operations were carried out with these troops who had been in trenches and moving from one position to another, no Reserve troops, for 8 days & 8 nights. All officers behaved magnificently. Their casualties were very severe. — 370 NCOs & men + 15 officers — Major Hobbs missing. He was seen wounded in the shoulder in the communication trench, he came out of the trench + twice went up to rescue people. The whistle blew + he was carried by stretcher bearers in the night. 2nd Lt Nott & 3 Sergeants attd. died of wounds + others (Bomb wounds & Shrapnel) Capts & Lieuts very severely wounded in the head.	

Army Form C. 2118.

WAR DIARY
or
INTELLIGENCE SUMMARY

(Erase heading not required.)

Instructions regarding War Diaries and Intelligence Summaries are contained in F.S. Regs., Part II. and the Staff Manual respectively. Title pages will be prepared in manuscript.

Hour, Date, Place	Summary of Events and Information	Remarks and references to Appendices
2nd Oct 1915 (cont)	Lt Weber badly wounded in the right forearm, remaining with his M.G. all night, though wounded, until relieved from D.T.O. Capt Warren wounded & a prisoner. The following officers were casualties :— Major A.H. Robbs missing Capt J.L.E. Warren — " — 2/Lt Morse R.P. Wounded — " Davies G. Missing " Davies T.J.C. Wounded — some doubt — " White H.T. — " — " Pope P.P. — " — " Head R.D. — " — Lt Vincent C. — " — Lt Kensington S. — " — 2/Lt Weber C.T. — " — Capt Egerton G.W. — " — 2/Lt Hazell M. Missing 2/Lt Lord A. Wounded Lt Toller R.A. — " —	

WAR DIARY
INTELLIGENCE SUMMARY

Army Form C. 2118.

Hour, Date, Place	Summary of Events and Information	Remarks and references to Appendices
3rd October 1915	Relieved from Old British Front Line Trench and marched back to VERMELLES. At 7pm 2nd Lt Morgan was taken to hospital suffering from rheumatism. Capt. W. Owen assumed command.	
4th	Battn occupied Sussex Trench – VERMELLES.	
5th	Battn marched to ANNEQUIN to Billets.	
6th	Battn marches to BETHUNE – Billeted in the Orphanage.	
7th	Battn marches to LA PIERRIÈRE and billeted in farms.	
8th to 18th	In Billets at LA PIERRIÈRE.	
18th	Battn left at 8am and marched to LES HARRESOIRS and billeted.	
19th	Battn marched to BETHUNE and billeted.	
20th	In Billets at Bethune.	

www.ingramcontent.com/pod-product-compliance
Lightning Source LLC
Chambersburg PA
CBHW081241170426
43191CB00034B/2005